# BONE SKIN FLESH

# 骨皮肉

Balestier Press
Centurion House, London TW18 4AX
www.balestier.com

*Bone Skin Flesh* 骨皮肉
Copyright © 顏艾琳 Yen Ai Lin, 1997; 2018
English translation © Jenn Marie Nunes, 2025
English translation based on the 2018 edition in Traditional Chinese.

Photography © 顏艾琳 Yen Ai Lin

This bilingual edition first published by Balestier Press in 2025.

臺灣總代理發行：島座放送 ISLANDSET Co., Ltd.

Published with the support of the Ministry of Culture, Taiwan.

A CIP catalogue record for this book is available from the British Library.

ISBN 978 1 913891 63 3

Cover art: *Lace Calligraphy* by 洪慧 Hong Wai
Cover visual concept by 黃千芮 Connie Huang

All rights reserved. No part of this publication may be reproduced, stored in a retrieval system, or transmitted in any form or by any means, electronic or mechanical, without prior written permission from the publisher.

YEN AI LIN
顏艾琳

# BONE SKIN FLESH
骨皮肉

*Translated from the Chinese by*
Jenn Marie Nunes

BALESTIER PRESS
LONDON · SINGAPORE

# Contents

| | | |
|---|---|---|
| | 9 | *Translator's Preface* |

## 一
## 黑暗溫泉

## I
## Dark Hot Springs

| | | |
|---|---|---|
| 獸 | 16 | Animal |
| 度冬的情獸 | 18 | Wintering Love Animals |
| 塊狀欲望 | 20 | The Stuff of Desire |
| 黑暗溫泉 | 22 | Dark Hot Springs |
| 水性 | 24 | Aqueous |
| 淫時之月 | 28 | Wee Hours of the Moon |
| 善後工作 | 30 | Aftermath |
| 飢餓的夜 | 32 | Hungry Night |

## 二
## 單性情人日

## II
## Single on Valentine's Day

| | | |
|---|---|---|
| 史前記憶 | 38 | Prehistoric Memory |
| 衣服的聯想 | 40 | Clothing Connotations |
| 瑪麗蓮夢露 | 42 | Marilyn Monroe |
| 單性情人日 | 44 | Single on Valentine's Day |
| 青春期與其後 | 48 | Puberty and Beyond |
| 亞當的蘋果核 | 52 | Adam's Apple Core |
| 孤獨城堡 | 56 | Solitary Castle |
| 食耳 | 58 | Earful |

## 三
## 超級販賣機

| | | |
|---|---|---|
| 速度 | 64 | Speed |
| 劇場 | 66 | Theater |
| 超級販賣機 | 68 | Super Vending Machine |
| 魘事 | 70 | The Stuff of Nightmares |
| 巨鯨的自卑論 | 72 | Whale's Inferiority Complex |
| 虛無之調 | 74 | In the Key of Nothingness |
| 關於道德二則 | 76 | Two Principles of Morality |
| 夜的兩種說法 | 78 | Two Ways of Saying Night |

## 四
## 空體賦

| | | |
|---|---|---|
| 上去或下來 | 84 | Going Up or Coming Down |
| 探測一朵蘭花的心意 | 86 | Detecting an Orchid's Intent |
| 午夜索隱 | 88 | Midnight's Secret |
| 未成品裝潢 | 90 | Minor Adornments |
| 關於憂鬱 | 92 | Regarding Melancholy |
| 夜裡城堡 | 94 | Night Castle |
| 空體賦 | 98 | Empty Body |

## 五
## 隱隱燃

| | | |
|---|---|---|
| 隱隱燃 | 106 | Faint Spark |
| 寒食 | 108 | Cold Food Festival |
| 抽象三圖 | 110 | Three Abstract Images |
| 流浪漢 | 112 | Vagrant |

| | | |
|---|---|---|
| 暑雨 | 114 | Summer Rain |
| 星期五、禮拜二 以及星期日 | 116 | Friday, Tuesday, and Sunday |
| 她們被夢著 | 118 | They've Been Dreamed |
| 暗夜 | 120 | Dark Night |
| 黑牡丹 | 122 | Black Peony |
| 雛樹 | 124 | Sapling |
| 迷路的基因 | 126 | Gene for Getting Lost |
| 慾望在夜的暗潮，上岸 | 128 | Desire, in the Undercurrent of Night, Washes Ashore |

## 六
## 寄給憂鬱的一封信

## VI
## A Letter to Melancholy

| | | |
|---|---|---|
| 後來，以後 | 134 | After That, After This |
| 蚌 | 136 | Clam |
| 寄給憂鬱的一封信 | 138 | A Letter to Melancholy |
| 鬧鐘 | 140 | Alarm Clock |
| 冷茶心情 | 142 | An Iced Tea Mood |
| 蟹居 | 144 | Crab Shell |
| 寂寞一種 | 146 | One Kind of Loneliness |
| 梅雨 | 148 | Monsoon Season |
| | 153 | *About the Author* |
| | 155 | *About the Translator* |

*Translator's Preface*

THE VERY MOMENT Yen Ai-lin breezed into the café off Chifeng St., near the Zhongshan station, I was in. In black boots and a draping black blouse—somehow both dramatic and understated—her presence, much like Wallace Stevens's jar, took dominion everywhere. At the time, she was there to talk to me about her role as a judge for the annual migrant worker poetry contests run by the Taipei government, a key part of my dissertation research. She was the only person associated with the contests who had responded to my desperate Facebook messages, and her willingness to offer me her time meant that, while I was primarily showing up as a scholar interested in what she could tell me about other poets, I had also read some of her poetry. I had prepared a list of questions about her writing, partly because surely her identity as a poet was entwined with her identity as a judge of poetry. I wanted to honor that identity, because I could tell immediately—even from our relatively brief early exchanges—that she was thoroughly a poet.

And also, I was intrigued.

From what I'd read online, she was a poet who, like me, was not afraid of the label "woman poet." It did not limit her. It would be naïve to say the label is never intended to limit, but the tension it creates—the sometimes angry negotiation between how the world wants to define us and who we want to be—has, for me, been a generative space, a juicy, sometimes bloody site of possibility. I felt Ai-lin might say the same.

The same but different. Clearly, I can't write about Yen's work without writing about myself. There is a closeness I feel with her writing that has made translating this collection a profound and sticky pleasure. Yen is well-known in Taiwan for her poetry's unabashed exploration of the feminine, particularly poignant in 1997 when *Bone Skin Flesh* was first published. Now, these poems enter the English language—I hope—with a frank voice and stunning imagistic turns, reveling in the feminine in ways comfortingly familiar and urgently unexpected. As a poet myself invested in writing a queer female desire both exuberant and deadly serious, translating Yen's work has felt like a homecoming:

"My animal self and its animal self meet.
Gradually, I feel it invade"
我的神經與它的神經接通了,
漸漸,感覺它的侵占.

Yet these are her poems, not my own. Sometimes, the sticky work of translation comes from a lack of understanding or the space between languages, and sometimes, it comes from a kind of closeness. When Yen completely nails an image that has particular emotional resonance for me, I have to consider how to render it in English in a way that honors the experience and voice of poet and translator. I have to remember it is not my image.

The first line in "Hungry Night" is a small example of one of these moments: 夜深得有點透藍了. The first time I read this line, I felt the top of my head open like a flower. The night sky she is describing, the quality of dark and blue, is my favorite color and my favorite fleeting moment of the day, carrying a host of memories and emotions. I have tried to describe this quality in my own poetry and been unable to. Talking with Yen about it over lunch, trying to determine if what I was seeing and feeling also felt right to her, I got so excited I lost my Chinese and tried to communicate the texture of the sky with my fingers. She seemed just as excited. It felt like we were seeing the same sky.

I think there are many ways to translate this line, but I reached for something concentrated, the way I experience her image:

"Night's depths thick with blue." I chose to focus on that tangible quality, the depth that blue reveals at night, when black flattens. I resisted the urge to overwrite, to push more of myself into the line, although it is still shaped by my choices. I kept it grounded in my conversation with Yen and the energy between us as I tried to pull the feeling her words gave me out of the air over our lunch plates with my fingers.

This tangible quality—the texture not just of the body and the world through which a body moves, but also of the body's desires, of emotions, of waking and dreaming—is another sticky pleasure in Yen's poetry: the body turns an oozing filthy yellow beneath an assessing gaze, desire clogs the small intestine, the sky becomes a huge breast leaking copious mother-love, truth a glob of spit between a gossip's teeth, and the moon tonguing the erect skyscrapers…raises every penis's longing for home. Yen's poetry makes new worlds—or new ways to feel this world. Her poems do not flow over you—they grow in you, on you, out of you. I wouldn't call her poetry maximalist, but it has a way of taking up space, of proliferating beyond the page.

The felt nature of the poems in *Bone Skin Flesh*, in conjunction with the way women figure in them—across ages, bold and uncertain, fleshy and the stuff of dreams—the way their bodies, desires, and accoutrements loom large, makes Yen feel like a Taiwanese sibling in the *Gurlesque*—a term conjured by Arielle Greenberg and Lara Glenum that "describes writers who perform femininity in their poems in a campy or overtly mocking manner, risking the grotesque to shake the foundations of acceptable female behavior and language." In other words, a poetics that turns again and again to the feminine even and especially in ways and when the world has told it to stop.

Perhaps it's the time Yen spent as a keyboard player for a punk band that gives her vividly crafted imagery a *riot grrrl* edge, makes her poems sticky with embodied sensation, and yet buoys them up with a persistently playful turn towards pleasure. Just as "fun, subversive, and important" as the writing by Gurlesque poets, Yen's work also has a certain tenderness, a punk earnestness, even a reverence for the feminine in the form of the mother, the lover, the crone, as well as in the loneliness and melancholy they might all share, that the Gurlesque does not tend to lean into. "Back back and forth forth," her poetry swings between "youth's desire soaked body" and "an empty ovary hanging in the lower abdomen," between the objectification and commodification of Marilyn Monroe and the vision of a whale as "just a little dollop of / sperm in an ocean," and between a "half tongue lolling from kissed lips, / skin awash in a deluge of sweat" and the "the depths of a great darkness" where "blooms a black peony that will eat / your heart."

Again, I know these poems, and I do not.

Regardless, Yen's poetry in this book did not feel difficult to translate. Sure, it took time. Sometimes I had to sit and listen, my fingers working in the air, before the words would come. And it took back and forth with Yen, who understood that I often just needed her to say more about an image, to contextualize it in her imaginary, who knew when I wasn't getting a reference—often to Buddhism—and who continued to be just as generous with her time and resources as she had been from day one. I don't want to say much else about these poems, because as a poet, I don't think poetry need be explained. In my work as a scholar of translation, I have often pushed to open up more room for the translator to be seen, to be visible, often in dramatic and experimental ways. That is not the work I have done with these poems. But I want it to be clear that I am in these translations—that is the way translations are—and so I have tried to point to some of the places where I meet Yen's work. Because these are also Yen's poems. I want to leave plenty of room for you to meet them where you will.

*Jenn Marie Nunes*
*January 2025*

# BONE SKIN FLESH
# 骨皮肉

Poetry 詩 / Photography 攝影
顏艾琳 Yen Ai Lin

English Translation 英譯
Jenn Marie Nunes

# I
# 黑暗溫泉
# Dark Hot Springs

# 獸

情人帶來一隻獸,
叫我輕撫它的脊椎骨。
它的毛髮以溫柔
來回饋我易滿足的觸覺
……後來
我的神經與它的神經接通了,
漸漸,感覺它的侵占。

我向情人呼喊:「
它消化我了……」

情人卻用一種愚人節的微笑
看著我無法抵抗,
而被一隻以愛情飼養的寵物
所吞噬。

:「夜,
謝謝你啣住了她的情緒。」於是
我的情人在過後不久
便無法控制
那隻巨大且狂野且黑沉且柔情的
獸。

## Animal

Lover brings an animal,
tells me to caress its spine.
Back and forth, its hair's softness
gifts me a satisfied touch
…… After
my animal self and its animal self meet.

Gradually, I feel it invade.

I yell to lover: "
It's consumed me……"
Lover only gives a little April Fool's Day smile,
watching me unable to resist
being swallowed by a pet raised solely
on love.

"Night,
thank you for holding her emotions in your mouth." And so
my lover not much later
is unable to control
that enormous, wild, cave-dark and tender
animal.

## 度冬的情獸

冬天的時候
我們窩在棉被的巢裏,
獸一般地取暖。
親愛的小孩,
你貪心地吸吮我的乳房
含糊而濕濡地說
:「你的雙乳很原始、
　你的奶頭很古典、
　你的體溫很東方……」
是的,我們臥姿
是洪荒時期取火的動作,
藉由摩擦和不斷地鑽抽
來燃燒自己的文明。

親愛的小孩,
睡意來襲之前
我們都是「更新世」的野獸,
還在渴望著直立的生活。

但,我們還是蜷躺著吧!
用肉體建築最初的洞穴,
潛躲我們害羞而不可告人的進化。

## Wintering Love Animals

In winter
we burrow in the nest of blankets,
like animals seeking warmth.
Dearest child,
you greedily suck my nipple,
wet mouthing, as if to say
: "Your two breasts are so primitive,
   your nipples so classical,
   your temperature so Eastern ......"
Yes, our position
is a primitive act seeking fire
through friction, endlessly mining
our own civility for fuel.

Dearest child,
before sleepiness attacks
we're both Pleistocene creatures,
still longing for a life erect.

But let's stay curled in bed!
Use flesh to build the first cave,
conceal our reluctant evolution.

## 塊狀欲望

愛情非霜淇淋。
你說,也不全然固定
或者流動

那麼,在這間小小的房裡,
空氣中填塞的是什麼?

狡黠的你賊賊答我:
欲望是甜的,
而房間是方糖。
因此,
我們互相調劑
彼此的體味

## The Stuff of Desire

Love is not soft-serve.
And yet it's not entirely set, you say,
nor free flowing

Then in this tiny little room,
what is it that stuffs the air?

Sly you and your wily reply:
Desire is sweet
and the room a sugar cube.
So
we join in twisting up
the taste of our bodies

## 黑暗溫泉

如果生活很累
道德很輕,
那麼,
卸下一切
投入黑暗中吧!

黑暗中的底層
是我在等待。
為了誘引你的到來
我將空氣搓揉——
成秋天森林的乾爽氣味,
適合助燃
我們燃點很低的肉體。

讓你來汲取我的溫潤吧!
即使再深的疲倦
都將在黑暗的溫泉裏,
洗褪。

## Dark Hot Springs

If life is so tired
and virtue so light,
then,
take it all and
toss it into the black!

The bottom of the darkness
is me waiting
to tempt you down.
I'll stroke the air into
autumn forest's crisp breath,
ready to set alight
our smoldering flesh.

Come draw from my depths!
Even if your exhaustion runs deeper,
all is washed away in my dark
hot springs.

# 水性——女子但書

「道德是一件易脫的內衣,」
「不過是貼己的褻物而已。」

## 沐

年輕時就被慾望浸濕過的胴體
像株害羞的植物,
只盡在自身裡演化著年齡,
而遲遲不肯結些果子

即使花季逐年凋零
今年的花一如去歲的容顏,
仍將貞操再次複製。

## 潮

日子剛過去,
經血沖洗過的子宮
現在很虛無地鬧著飢餓;
沒有守寡的卵子
也沒有來訪的精子。
只剩一個
吊在腹腔下方的空巢,
無父無母、
無子無孫。

**渡**

很早很早的早晨
是
很晚很晚的黑夜

慾望在雙乳之間擱淺
很無趣地擺盪著；
從非常遠的早晨
擺渡到非常近的晚上,
反反覆覆
早早晚晚

## Aqueous—Woman's Proviso

*"Morality is a pair of easily shed underwear,
just an intimate obscenity."*

*Bathe*

Youth's desire-soaked body
like a tree's shy trunk,
insides flush with the evolutions of age,
but slow slow to give fruit

Even though youth's blooms wither every year,
this year's flowers have the look of last year's,
still chastely another copy.

*Flow*

Those days are gone,
uterus flushed of menses
now empty, clamoring with hunger.
There's no last widowed ova
and no sperm come to visit.
All that's left is one
empty ovary hanging in the lower abdomen,
No father no mother,
no sons no grandsons.

*Ferry*

Early early in the morning
is
late late in the night

Desire stranded between breasts
dully swinging.
From such a distant morning,
stroke by stroke to this near evening,
back back and forth forth
early early and late late

## 淫時之月

骯髒而淫穢的桔月升起了。
在吸滿了太陽的精光氣色之後
她以淺淺的下弦

微笑地，
舔著雲朵
舔著勃起的高樓
舔著矗立的山勢；

以她挑逗的唇勾
撩起所有陽物的鄉愁。

## Wee Hours of the Moon

A filthy, wanton sliver of moon rises.
Once she's suckled full on the sun's wan face,
her shallow waning crescent

a wee grin,
tonguing the clouds
tonguing the erect skyscrapers
tonguing the towering mountain range

with teasing lips,
she raises every penis's longing for home

# 善後工作

我們必須收拾
因過多浪費的欲望；
在餐桌上的狼藉。
義大利麵撐滿我的迴腸、
起士和牛油竄進血液裡……
吃食過多，
以使我產生噁心的感覺

我們還必須收拾
因恣意放縱的欲望；
在床褥之間的凌亂。
被親吻的嘴所吐出的半截舌頭、
氾濫的汗水沖刷大片的肌膚、
決堤的黏液等等……

像收拾餐桌一樣
即使過飽而感覺油膩，
仍要恢復乾淨，
期待下一次的飢餓
及享用！

## Aftermath

We'd better tidy up
all this wasted desire,
the ravaged tabletop.
Spaghetti clogs my small intestine,
cheese and oil flood the blood……
Gluttony,
it makes me sick

We still need to tidy up
this unbridled, indulgent desire,
a mess between the sheets.
Half tongue lolling from kissed lips,
skin awash in a deluge of sweat,
a sticky breach……

Just like clearing a table,
even if I'm full and feeling greasy,
I should still be reset to clean,
primed for the next hunger
that wants to use me!

## 飢餓的夜

夜深得有點透藍了。
失眠的胃
如同失眠的眼,
在搜尋一盤對味的夢境。
我明瞭飢餓是一種偽善
挑嘴,而妄想成為
清心寡欲的修行者。

封建式的胃,
使我對糧食的記憶
越來越淡薄。
是的。
夜只有一個
並且即將逝去,
但我的飢餓
卻一直會持續下去,
直到你甜美的黑皮膚
覆蓋我的雙眼,
金屬一般且彈性的肌里
咀嚼在脣齒之間,
而你韌性十足的心
在我空洞的胃裡……
我才能在睡遲的早上,
打一個氣嗝
說:「晚安。」

# Hungry Night

Night's depths thick with blue.
Sleepless stomach
like sleepless eyes,
searching for a tempting plate of dreams.
I know picky hunger is a kind of
hypocrite, and delusion
an unshorn monk free from desire.

Tyrant stomach,
making my memory of food
more and more bland.
Really.
Night just has one
and it's on the verge of death,
but my hunger
will always press on,
until the sweet depths of your skin
cover my two eyes,
skin like gold, yet supple
between the teeth,
and your constant heart
in my cave-empty stomach......
It's late in the morning when I at last
hiccup out
a "Good night."

# II
# 單性情人日
## Single on Valentine's Day

# 史前記憶

天好藍
，藍過我的憂鬱了
，於是
不得不快樂
……

非假寐不可
，以消除夢的沉疴
（一種虛偽的幸福感。）
孤獨嗎
？孤獨
。我不睡雙人床
，那會養成一種非非的壞習慣

這樣的藍
純潔得不帶任何心情
：然
，出現在如此多元進化的城市叢林中
我被迫還原成
史前一枚沉睡的
：貝
。

# Prehistoric Memory

Sky so blue
, a blue beyond my melancholy
, that
I can't not be happy
……

I've got to take a little nap
, to dispel the chronic sick of dreams
(a kind of false sense of well-being.)
Lonely
? Lonely
. I don't sleep a double bed
, that would make for a rotten habit

This blue
so pure it carries no connotation
: then
, to appear amidst this teeming urban forest
it presses me all the way back into
a prehistoric pearl of sodden sleep
: a clam
.

## 衣服的聯想

這件百分之百的羊毛衫
使我保持溫暖,
也包裹著我的心、
柔化了冬夜裡的傷痛。

剝去生活熱情的屠夫,
在另一個豐滿女子的被窩中
狡獸般地靠情欲取暖;
而形同赤裸地坦陳沮喪的我,
學會溫馴地披上羊毛衫,
不再輕易地
讓人測量體溫……

## Clothing Connotations

This one-hundred percent wool shirt
keeps me warm.
It envelops my heart,
softening winter's ache.

You've stripped away my passion for life, killer of love,
and like a cunning animal warm yourself on lust
in another woman's lush amongst the blankets;
while practically naked with dismay, I
learn to meekly cloak myself in a woolen shirt.
No one will easily
gauge my temperature again……

## 瑪麗蓮夢露

「這裡躺的是瑪麗蓮夢露。 36.24.36 」
　　　　　　　　　　——摘自其墓誌銘


A教授推上滑落的眼鏡，
慎重地告訴我：
其實，瑪麗蓮夢露
是純粹普普主義的作品。

第二次世界大戰以後，
可口可樂的瓶子
便大大流行起來，
這同夢露的三圍
有著相當的關聯。
據說：
有些男子，利用可口可樂的瓶子——
自慰並射精……

難怪夢露自殺

# Marilyn Monroe

*"Here lies Marilyn Monroe. 36, 24, 36"*
    —Taken from the inscription on her grave

Professor A pushes up the glasses sliding down his nose
and informs me:
Actually, Marilyn Monroe
is purely an artifact of the pop art movement.

After World War II,
Coca-Cola bottles
became hugely popular,
having proportions similar
to Monroe's measurements.
It is said:
There are some men who used Coca-Cola bottles——
to jerk off……

No wonder Monroe killed herself

# 單性情人日

**景1**

雨下的令我吃驚。

**景2**

太多太多的水。
天空彷彿在生一種異常任性的怨氣
沒有預兆顯示
便哭得地上那條巨大的手帕
來不及捻乾,
又濕,又濕,

**景3**

一隻被雨刷洗得太過蒼白的小獸
匆匆忙忙逃向最近的遮蔽物內
企圖躲過雨水們鍥而不捨的追捕

**景4**

回到室內的小獸,
漸漸瀝乾狼狽的形像後,
才恢復「我」人體原來的線條。

景5

為了取暖
我緊緊抱住受潮的身影
在夜色逐次上漲的一隅中
雕塑成一塊凝重的岩石


景6

無端；更冷。


景7

竟夜因強烈的憂鬱氣團不散
心情哆嗦直到晨光從山上行來窗前
拉起我那假想的雄性影子，
掛過雌性肉體的挽留
步向充滿鳥聲的戶外天地。


景8

天氣好得足以讓我快樂一整天
雖然；


景9

雖然；
天氣好得足以讓我快樂一整天

# Single on Valentine's Day

*Scene 1*

The rainfall caught me by surprise.

*Scene 2*

Way way too much water.
As if the sky, in delivering some exceptionally strong grievance,
without a sign of warning,
sobs into the wide handkerchief of earth,
wetter and wetter,
without a moment wrung dry,

*Scene 3*

A little beast, scrubbed too pale by the rain,
hurriedly flees toward the closest shelter,
trying to take cover before the water's relentless onslaught

*Scene 4*

Back inside, the bedraggled little beast,
once it has gradually dripped dry,
is finally restored to its original human form: "me"

*Scene 5*

In order to get warm
I tightly hug my damp self
in that corner where night's darkness gradually rises
a statue becomes a piece of solemn stone


*Scene 6*

For some reason; it's colder.


*Scene 7*

Because this violent mass of air sticks around all night,
my mood wavers until dawn shines from mountain peaks before
   the window,
tugs at my false male shadow,
my female body's urge to stay suspended,
I step out toward a birdsong world.


*Scene 8*

The weather is good enough to make me happy all day
and yet,


*Scene 9*

And yet,
the weather is good enough to make me happy all day

## 青春期與其後

**青春期**

我們活在「公民與道德」之中。
比「健康教育」還害羞多了。
並且,
支付彼此未成熟的憂傷

那些憂傷因尚未被世俗染色,而
在我們的眼裡
剔透地閃著:
不為人知的欲念。

**車位**

那女子的靦腆
用驕傲裝飾著,
像一隻貓模糊的嘟噥
:「在他擁擠的心裡,
有我的一塊黃金地段。」

真的,我善良得沒有告訴她,
自一九八八年四月,
我早把他廉售給另一位女子;
那時,
他已經在心的空地上,
建好一座巨大停車場。

**作夢**

今夜,
我準備用心雕塑一個古典的夢,
穿上中世紀的公主服,故意去尋一隻噴火恐龍;
溫柔地請求牠
:「擄獲我。」
然後再看看那個不怕燒烤的厚臉皮,
竟敢潛入我的夢中,
冒充白馬王子,
以拯救他的美夢?

**數羊後遺症**

鄰室的妹妹搖著木牆說
:「數一數那略帶神經質的
咩咩叫的小羊群吧!
再不數,
牠們都要因而失眠了⋯⋯」

**青梅竹馬**

有太多不該有的浪漫,
被我和他,
支付在一次
因於年紀貧窮的愛情裡。

廿一歲,
他心不甘情不願地,
很成人儀式地對我說
:「　　我愛妳　。」
我的心,
隨著他不高不低的語調,
落下了童年最後一次
撒嬌的,淚

# Puberty and Beyond

*Puberty*

We live between *civic* and *virtue*.
Shier even than *health education*.
What's more,
we pay for each other's immature sorrows,

those sorrows not yet tainted by the wide world, and so
in our eyes
sparking brightly:
unfathomed desire

*Parking Spot*

That woman's timidity
adorned with pride,
like a cat's low hum
: "There in his crowded heart
is my square of prime real estate."

Really, it's kind I haven't told her
that by April 1988,
I'd sold him fair and square to another woman.
At that time,
he'd already built a huge parking lot
in the empty place in his heart

*To Dream*

This evening,
I prepare a carefully crafted classical dream,
put on a princess gown from the Middle Ages, search out a fire-breathing dragon,
demurely request that it
"Take me."
Then I take another look at that brazen man, unafraid of a roasting,
daring to slip himself into my dreams,
pretending to be a knight on a white horse,
just to protect his own fantasy?

*After-Effects of Counting Sheep*

The young girl next door hammers on the wooden wall saying
: "Count that anxious little group of
Baa-baa-baa-ing sheep, will you!
Don't count them and
they'll all lose sleep…"

*Green Plums and Bamboo Horses*

There's too much romance that shouldn't be,
by him and me.
Paying for it once again
because in this age love is deficient.

Twenty-one years old,
he says to me stiffly,
like performing a rite of passage
: "I love you."
My heart,
following his flat tone,
shed's youth's very last
coquettish tear

## 亞當的蘋果核

她削著蘋果，
用蜂蜜一般的聲音
灌入我的耳朵。

「真受不了呀！
我跟吸血鬼同樣愛啃人家的
——脖子。」
她是愛情的老饕；
「尤其是男生的喉結……」
她結論著。

## Adam's Apple Core

She peels an apple,
pours her honey-like
voice into my ear.

"I really can't stand it!
Same as a vampire, I love to bite
necks."
She is love's glutton;
"Especially men's Adam's apples…"
she concludes

## 孤獨城堡

誠徵男伴。擅熱鬧、嬉戲。
　　　　　——城主　啟

患上同類型的病友
都離得不遠不近；
恰好是出了門會覺得疲倦的距離，
因此誰也不去探望誰，
每個人都窩在私屬的城堡裡。
偶然想起誰說過的笑話
就當是莫大的溫暖。

我們是孤獨的伯爵、
與寂寞的王侯子弟，
枯瘦的身軀
不易被庸俗的話題點燃笑意。
而我們的城堡，
大且虛幻
虛幻且堅固
堅固又溫柔地包圍我們，
給我們無微不至的呵護；
習慣它的冷
以及豐富的魔術身段。以及
常常忘了世界。

常常忘了自己也是肉身，
需要七情六慾的餵食。

只吸吮月光、雲氣、
及囫圇吞進的大片夜色。
但我的城堡會營養我，
供我消化更多的文字與圖像。

要跟你說的是：
孤獨城堡是超意識的建築，
被攜帶著四處走逛、
隨地坐落
讓我立即隔絕過多的無聊
或，虛偽的熱情。
它成就一種情性潔癖的修行。

最近覺得；
我的城堡又長大了，
那空間增加一個馬戲團。
有印度白象、台灣彌猴、
海豚、亞馬遜巨蟒、
北極熊、美洲豹、
非洲獅、北歐馴鹿、
澳大利亞袋鼠、四川熊貓……
還有上百種遊樂設施，
龐大的遊戲區
延伸到不忍獨享的況境。
因此，
我開了扇窗，
不要告訴別人
我曾邀請你來城堡玩耍。

趕快爬上來吧，
城堡是沒有門的……

## Solitary Castle

*Wanted, male companion. Good at fun and games.*
*— Keeper of the Castle*

Patients all suffering the same malady,
none too far or too close.
Turns out, it's tired-from-stepping-out-the-door distance,
meaning no one goes to visit anyone,
everyone stays holed up in their solitary castles.
Occasionally thinking of a joke someone told,
is the greatest source of warmth.

We are solitary earls
and lonely aristocrats,
withered bodies
hardly sparked to smiles by vulgar topics.
And our castles,
big and illusory,
illusory and solid,
solid, they softly surround us,
take care of our every need.
We're accustomed to the cold
and the rich magic ways. And
often we forget the world.

Often we forget we are bodies,
and must feed our human needs.

We drink moonlight, cloud wisp,
swallow whole big swathes of night.
But my castle can sustain me,
supply me with more words and images to digest.

What I want to say is:
The solitary castle is psychic architecture,
carried along anywhere I roam.
Anywhere I sit,
it immediately separates me from boredom
or tricky passions.
It's become a kind of devotee to clean emotion.

Lately, I think:
My castle has grown up again.
That space has added a circus
with Indian elephants, Taiwanese macaques,
dolphins, Amazonian pythons,
polar bears, panthers,
African lions, reindeer,
Australian kangaroos, Sichuan pandas......
And over a hundred kinds of rides,
an enormous playground,
stretching past the point of solitary fun.
Thus,
I open the shutters.
Don't tell anyone else
I've invited you specially to come in and play.

Quick, climb up.
The castle has no door......

# 食耳

「感覺要吞下一個謊言
　原來是這樣地快樂……」

親愛的,今夜我決定吃掉你的耳朵。
想必在我長期甜言蜜語的釀造下,
那耳根應當香香脆脆,
肥嫩的耳垂嚼感十足……
於是我逐漸湊近你,
持著銳利的初六月光
迅速割下熟睡中的耳殼。

你忽然自深濃的夢裡
汎至清醒的岸上,
見了我貪婪咀嚼的模樣,只
一慣輕柔地問我
：「好吃嗎？」
我吞嚥著一個又一個
傾倒而出的謊話；
為以前放入太多
導致我們愛情虛胖的甜份,
而哽咽起來……

# Earful

*"Feeling like you should swallow down a lie
Ah, so it's that kind of happiness......"*

Dearest, tonight I've decided to eat up your ear.
Brewed so long in my sweet nothings,
the ear root should be fragrant and crisp,
the fat, tender lobe a perfect chew......
So I slowly lean in,
wielding the sharp light of early June
and quick cut off an ear while you sleep.

Suddenly, from the thick depths of dream
you swim to the shores of wakefulness,
catch me chewing greedily, and
fondly ask
: "Taste good?"
I swallow one and then another
lie as it pours out;
putting too many in
led to our love's bloated sweetness,
and I choke on the sobs......

# III
# 超級販賣機
## Super Vending Machine

## 速度

山,退後
樹,退後
雲,退後
河,退後
人,退後
高樓退後
霓虹退後
夕陽退後
馬路退後
愛情退後
悲歡退後
歷史退後
…………
…………
時光退後
在一四○的指數上
我駕馭著速度
如此看見
　唯我
　　前
　　進
　　　。

## Speed

      Mountains, recede
      Trees, recede
      Clouds, recede
      Rivers, recede
      People, recede
      Skyscrapers recede
      Rainbows recede
      Sunsets recede
      Streets recede
      Love recedes
      Pessimism recedes
      History recedes
      ............
      ............
      Time recedes
At a rate of ninety miles per hour
   At the speed I'm driving
      It appears it's
        Only me
        Advanc
          ing

## 劇場

她說:「開一瓶十二歲的約翰走路吧!」
謝了幕之後,
男女主角都為結局悵然。
只有一群旁觀者清的第三人稱,
嗤著鼻子,以不屑的手勢
捻熄周圍的聚光燈。

他們卸了粧　戲服
假髮　情緒
表情　個性……
現實的習慣一一地匯入記憶裡。
最後,他們默契十足
挑選矯作的台詞:「

為——以往的合作,乾杯。」
陳年的液體
只短暫地通過喉嚨,
有一種帶著後勁的失望
醺然湧上心頭,

沒有人喊:安可。

# Theater

She says: "Open a 12-year-old bottle of Johnny Walker!"
After the curtain call,
the male and female lead are both disappointed with the ending.
All that's left is a group of onlookers
who with derisive snorts and disdainful gestures
flick off the spotlights.

They take off their make-up         costumes
                        wigs         emotions
                                expressions    personalities......
real habits gather one by one in their memories.
Lastly, with unspoken agreement they
choose to perform the lines: "

To—our work together, cheers."
The aged liquor
slips quick through throats.
There's a kind delayed disappointment
that drunkenly gushes over their hearts.

No one shouts: encore.

## 超級販賣機

我覺得飢渴。

我投下所有的錢,
它什麼也沒給我。

我只好把手腳給它

又將頭遞過去

但還不夠。

我繼續讓它吞噬其它的肢體,
它仍舊不給我任何東西。

最後我把靈魂也投給了它。
它吐出一副骸骨
並漠然顯示
「恕不找零」

# Super Vending Machine

I feel hungry and thirsty.

I drop in all my money,
and it gives me nothing.

I'd best give it my hands and feet

and hand over my head

but it's still not enough.

I continue to let it swallow my limbs,
but even then it won't give me a thing.

Finally, I take my soul and drop it in.
It spits out a skeleton
and mechanically blinks
"Sorry no change"

## 魘事

我們站在陽光下的陰影
其實居住著死神。
我們帶著祂,走來又走去
直到生命的盡路、
直到肉體很疲倦的時候,
祂才打開那張單薄的黑影,
用一雙比夜色更闇墨的手,
將我們的眼睛覆上。

永睡的瞳孔
看到我們原是生活在
死神的陰影裡……

## The Stuff of Nightmares

We stand in the shadow of the sun.
In fact, the god of death lives here.
We carry it, walking back and then forth
to the end of life's road,
until our bodies are exhausted.
It finally opens that thin black shadow,
and using two hands even blacker than night,
covers up our eyes.

Eternally sleeping pupils
see we've been living
in Death's shadow……

## 巨鯨的自卑論

牠濡濡地吐出泡沫,
掩飾臉部害羞的面積。
「在海洋裡,
我不過是人間的
一枚　微小精子。」

## Whale's Inferiority Complex

It spits out a gush of foam,
veiling the shy look of its face.
"In your world,
I'm just a little dollop of
sperm      in an ocean."

# 虛無之調

## 自行演奏

我仍穿著五十萬年來
沒什麼改進的肉體大衣,
長長短短的一生
揮霍在吃喝、消化、排泄
尋找人生目的和伴侶。
也許會遇上一次世界大戰
幾次經濟危機,
但我仍喜愛
睡眠、喝酒、作愛、洗澡。
世界亂了幾次

我還是一個有潔癖的地球人


## 一小節四拍 (4 / 4)

生命和死亡之間
保持一種馴良的距離

季節不過是
4 / 4 拍子的巡迴演出。

# In the Key of Nothingness

*Solo Performance*

I'm still wearing this 500,000-year-old
suit of flesh with no improvements.
Long or short, I spend life
in a flurry of eating, digesting, excreting,
looking for purpose and a partner.
Maybe I'll run into a world war,
a few economic crises,
but I'll still love
to sleep, drink, make love, bathe.
No matter how many times the world's in chaos

I'm still an earthling who has to be clean


*Four Beats in a Measure (4/4)*

Between life and death
maintain a gentle distance

The seasons are just
a tour in 4/4 time.

## 關於道德二則

膳

善良無異是一杯布丁；
適口的柔軟
使心腸消化成
一種甜蜜。

醉

矯正所有的傾斜，
眾人還是不可置信
——一個扶正的
我的樣子。

## Two Principles of Morality

*Food*

Kindness is no different than a cup of pudding;
a pleasant softness in the mouth
digests the heart into
a kind of sweetness.

*Drunk*

Straighten every slant,
still no one can believe
—my propped up
likeness.

## 夜的兩種說法

I

整條河都被黑夜傾注了。
今日的夜晚正漫漫往下游流去；
一些夢的泡沫
間　間　續　續
冒著囈語……


II

暗夜裡　天空一朵雲
我的廚房正煮著咖啡
灰色的雲在燠暑的氛圍中
彷彿比咖啡
還憂鬱許多
彷彿比喝咖啡
還哲學許多

# Two Ways of Saying Night

I

All the rivers are fed by night.
Today's night flows endlessly down;
some dreams foaming
on and on
risking nonsense……

II

In the dark night     a cloud in the sky
I happen to be boiling coffee in the kitchen
in the steamy atmosphere the grey cloud
seems much more melancholy
than coffee
it seems much more philosophical
than drinking coffee

# IV
# 空體賦
# Empty Body

## 上去或下來

當我感覺
季風已來到皮膚的陸地
將汗毛一根根植起
我正好立於樓梯中間。

沒有人教我
如此感覺季節
或是一些莫名的心情
竟會在脈搏裡跳繩
從頭頂到腳趾頭；

而我一爬上樓梯
世界的海拔和夜色
便漸漸漲了起來⋯⋯
候鳥的人字隊
帶著溫度計遷徙，
我仍站在不上不下的階梯
遲疑著；
迎接世紀末稀微的光芒
或則沉緬史前失真的記憶？

## Going Up or Coming Down

When I feel
the monsoon make landfall on my skin,
each fine hair by hair stand on end,
I happen to be halfway up a flight of stairs.

No one told me
I'd feel the season like this
or how these nameless feelings
would suddenly jump rope with my pulse
from crown to sole;

or how the moment I began to climb the steps
the dark nights, the world's heights
would begin to slowly swell......
A herringbone stitch of migratory birds
wing by carrying thermometers,
and I'm still standing motionless on the stairs
hesitating;
to welcome the century's last brilliant rays
or wallow in distant, distorted memories before time?

## 探測一朵蘭花的心意

看來,妳是有點老了。
但妳如此縱容地
讓懶散逐日為妳上色,
且把我的孤獨
芒雕在妳纖細的網脈上。

這麼仔細看來,
那漸萎的弧線
其實含有訕笑⋯⋯

## Detecting an Orchid's Intent

From here, it looks like you've aged.
Not only the way you've carelessly
let indolence become your finest feature,
but also how you've etched my loneliness
over the fine web of your veins.

But look closer,
and in that drooping arc,
a mocking smile……

## 午夜索隱

黑夜在窗外炸開來,
藉著晚風的身手
無聲地
在室內瀰漫、暈開。
彷彿是生活的色彩,
老在心版上
重重塗滿悲哀。

而憂鬱那顆星
一直躲在天空的南方,
要掉,卻掉不下來。
只曖昧地拋著冷光
告訴我:
「孤獨是一種清高、
一種對生命體認的饋賞。」
我笑了一笑
想了又想,低頭之間
便把黑夜吞了一塊。
「這明日的底餡
都曝光了呢!」
最後,我是這麼想。

# Midnight's Secret

Night bursts open outside the window,
borrows the wind's skill
and silently
fills the room with its dizzying stain.
Like the color of life,
a thick smear of sadness
long covering the page of my heart.

And that sullen star
always hiding in the southern skies,
wants to fall, but can't.
It just casts a cold, vague light,
and tells me:
"Loneliness is a virtue,
a kind of gift for seeing life as it is."
I smile a smile
and think for a bit. With head bowed
I swallow a piece of night.
"It's tomorrow's insides
all exposed!"
In the end, that's what I think.

## 未成品裝潢

莫要夜探我的睡姿，
那是一種你不懂的
幸福的象形。
偶爾，
剛剛出爐的
新鮮的夢，
被一群嗅覺靈敏的風追逐；
而我喜歡與他們分享
我那不為人知的秘密──
我的靈魂，
尚未雕刻完畢……

於是，為了裝飾這不完善，
我替它滾上一層
抒情、浪漫的蕾絲花邊，
給這件應該嚴肅而神聖的作品，
點綴一點點滑稽的線條。
然後我撕下一塊昨夜星辰包裹。
郵寄到你的夢裡：展覽。

## Minor Adornments

Don't spy on the shape of my sleeping body.
That's a pictogram of happiness
you don't understand.
Once in a while,
a dream fresh
from the oven,
is chased by keen-nosed winds;
I like to share with them
secrets not a single person knows—
my soul
is not yet fully formed……

So, to dress up this deficiency,
I roll on a romantic length
of lyrical lace.
I take what should be a serious, sacred work
and sprinkle in some comedic lines.
Then I tear down a swath of stars as wrapping,
and mail it to your dreams: For Display.

## 關於憂鬱

「上次是黃昏，
⋯⋯⋯⋯⋯，
⋯⋯⋯⋯⋯，
這次是深沉。」

你告別的台詞
未免太好了
使我思念的邏輯
不得不戲劇化一點。

「夕色可以燃盡，
但深沉呢？」

你說：
投海。

## Regarding Melancholy

"Last time was dusk,
......................,
......................,
This time it's night."

Your parting script
is a little too good.
Now the logic of my longing
can't help but up the drama.

"The evening sky can burn out,
but then there's my heavy heart."

You say:
*Throw it in the ocean.*

## 夜裡城堡

這是我對你說的枕邊童話　雖然
人人都知道它是謊言，
但　卻無法揭穿它⋯⋯

### 夜的邊陲

我會愛上一顆不被人喜歡的無名之星。
我甚至能夠忍受一個冷漠
或長距離的戀情；

因為，你天使的翅膀

### 方位之殞

夜。
　，在錯。綜。
　　複。雜。的。
　　　星。座。群。裡。
　　，遺。失。　　了。
一。　顆。
　　　北。　極。
　　　　　　　　　　星。

### 宵禁

門窗把夜的一部分關了進來，
你安全地睡著；
那些聒噪的星子靜得忘了眨眼。

而我自我的夢裡跨來，
攜帶一個午睡時，你忘了做的夢
為你輕輕地安上牀頭……

## 夢的題材

你說：「夢也都沉沉入睡了。」
以致於昨夜無夢。

那麼，
把我囚入夢的核心；
孵成一位童話人物吧！

## 仲夏之約

夏天的時候，
我躺在牀上的角度，
正好可以約會窗外的一顆星。

亮亮的；急著闖入夢中，
溯我意識流的上游，
和一些載浮載沉的夢想
玩淘金的遊戲。

## 夜　奔

在我醒了，　之後
一直疑問自己
：「　到底最後逃出來
　　　沒有？
　　　我，　和　你」

附記：夢是生活最後的牢籠、與最真的謊言，因而成此詩。

## Night Castle

*This is the bedtime story I'm telling you  Even though everyone knows it's a lie,*
  *still   there's no way to expose it......*

### The Edges of Night

I can fall in love with a nameless star no one likes.
I can even accept a distant
or detached love;

Because, your angel wings

### The Death of Directions

Night .
  , inside the .       Multitude .
   Of . Intricate .    And .
    Com . Plex . Star . Signs .
    , has . Loss .                Lost .
One .     Point .
   North .
                                         Star .

### Curfew

The doors and windows shut in a piece of night.
You're safely sleeping;
those noisy stars go so quiet they forget to blink.

And I stride out of my own dreams,
carrying a little nap, and carefully affix the dream
you forgot to dream to the headboard……

### Subject of the Dream

You say: "Dreams have all fallen into a deep sleep."
So that's why last night was dreamless.

In that case,
imprison me in the heart of a dream;
out will hatch a fairytale character!

### Midsummer Date

During summer,
the angle I lie in bed
is just right for engaging a star outside the window.

Shining bright, eager to break into dreams,
eddying in the upper reaches of my consciousness,
it plays at panning for gold with my dreams
as they bob along.

### Night Flight

In the moments after I wake,
I always ask myself
: "In the end do we escape
   or not?
   Me, and you"


Epilogue: dreams are life's last trap, and the truest lies, thus, this poem.

## 空體賦
——代序林群盛漫畫詩集《星舞絃獨角獸神話憶》

我知道,
布娃娃裡面填的是什麼。
不管是小熊、
小恐龍、
小胖豬、
饅頭娃娃,
還是受我暗戀的那個人,
他們不是渾然不知的東西。

在夜裡,
空氣聚集得比白天濃厚,
他們以夢做為交通工具,
出現在城市的上空,
笑瞇瞇地啃噬著建築體,
毫不費力地摧毀公共秩序,
或調皮地轟炸兒童樂園。
一切按卡通漫畫中的情節來遊戲。
就算有人被驚醒,
看見這所有超現實的畫面
也只會哦一聲:
「是夢。」
ZZZZZZZZ……

是夢。
布娃娃和失去勇氣的情人
在我的白天裡,

從來不敢造次；
他們裡面裝的是——
憑空想像的靈魂
與偶爾爆發的激情。
至於肉體，
不過是他們
美麗而無辜的裝飾，而已。

# Empty Body
—Preface to Lyra Girl's collection of manga poems *Legends of the Star Dancing Unicorn*


I know
what rag dolls are stuffed with.
Whether it's a teddy bear,
a little dragon,
a fat little pig,
a steam bun dolly,
or the person I'm secretly in love with.
They're not unknowable things.

At night,
air collects more thickly than day.
They use dreams as a means of transportation,
appearing in the sky above the city,
gnawing happily on buildings,
mischievously tossing TNT towards playgrounds,
carelessly destroying the public order.
Everything plays out like the plot in a cartoon.
Even if you were to awaken,
and see this absurd scene,
you'd just sigh out:
"A dream."
ZZZZZZZZZ…..

A dream.
Rag dolls and lovers who've lost their courage

in my day,
never dared be hasty;
their insides packed with—
a made up soul
accompanied by occasional passionate eruptions.
As for the flesh,
it's just a
pretty little decoration, nothing more.

# V
# 隱隱燃
# Faint Spark

## 隱隱燃

沒有嘴說話的女人
有一副很小、
很害羞的肩膀。
她的肢體和穿著
反映她心中的氣候

「冷。漠。
沒有人知道我的膽小
是因為過多的熱情
尚未點燃；
我等待那唯一的冒險。」
她緊閉的嘴
縮得跟腹腔類動物一樣；
很小。
而漠然的身軀
木木的，
彷彿在等人
將她削成一塊易燃的　柴。

# Faint Spark

A woman without a mouth to speak
has a pair of shy
little shoulders.
Her limbs and clothes
reflect the conditions in her heart.

"Cold. Indifferent.
No one knows my timidity
comes from an excess of passion
still unlit;
I'm waiting for that spark."
Her tightly closed mouth
shrunk up so small;
a sphincter-like animal.
And her wooden body
like sticks,
as if waiting for someone
to chop her into    kindling.

# 寒食

戰爭I　　戰爭II
槍砲　　原子彈
貧窮　　蕭條
傷痛　　悲涼
　高峰會議
　限武談判

餐桌上的羅列
（一群蒼蠅的翅膀
響在不遠處。）

倒了的酒
濺到用餐者雪白的圍巾上，
居然是……
　　血血血血血　　血血血‧‧
　　　血血血‧血　　　血血‧血
　　　　血血　血‧
　　　　　血　血血血‧　　血
　　血　　　血‧　血　　血
　　　　　　　‧血
　　　　血　血　　　血‧　血
　　　　　血　　　　血　血
　　　　‧　　　　血血血　血
　　　　　　‧　　　　　血
　　　　　　　血‧　　血
　　　　　　　　‧　　　血
的氾濫……………

## Cold Food Festival

WW I        WW II
guns         atomic bombs
poverty    desolation
pain         sorrow
  global summits
  armament talks

laid out on the dining room table
(A cloud of buzzing
flies hover nearby.)

Wine poured
splatters on a diner's snow-white scarf,
suddenly it's......
   blood blood blood blood blo  od   blood blo  od . .
     blood blo o  d . blood        blo  od blood. blood
       blood blood   blood.
         blood  blo od blood blood . blo
  o od        blood .   bloo o od
           . blood    blo
   oo      od      blood . blood
  blood            blood od
   .              blo  od  blo
            .           o od
           od .      blood
a flood..............

## 抽象三圖

作品No.1

寂寞是很輕的氛圍，
卻是一種沉重的
地心引力。
脫光衣服的女人
垂甸甸的雙乳在飲泣……
而梳妝臺上一朵玫瑰，
早已陽痿多時。

作品No.2

那個男人要打開一扇窗。
窗外的夕陽
像失去貞操的女人，
慘慘澹澹地
流洩滿眼的血紅。

作品No.3

一個小孩
用眼睛吶喊。
因為他的喉嚨
被「冷漠」打了結。

父親在十條街之外上班。
母親，是某醫院的大型植物。

# Three Abstract Images

*Piece No. 1*

Loneliness has a light touch,
but a very heavy
gravity.
A naked woman,
ponderous breasts crying silently......
And on her dressing table a single rose,
gone impotent long ago.

*Piece No. 2*

That man wants to open a window.
The setting sun beyond
like a woman whose virginity has been taken,
miserably painfully
eyes brim and run a bloody red.

*Piece No. 3*

A child
using eyes to shout.
Because his throat's
been knotted up by neglect.

His father at work outside a crossroads.
Mother, a giant plant in some hospital.

## 流浪漢

秋天的草
在他的頭頂蔓長起來,
他的雙眼乾涸
在枯索的外形下,
沒有人能秤知
他沉重而營養的靈魂;
只看出一種飢餓的象徵,
以他突出的肋骨
書寫在鬆皺的皮膚上。

是誰辜負了他?
還是誰
使他如此地辜負自己?
或則該給予施捨的我們,
早就拒絕他的存在?
只見他仍以禮貌的情緒
攪著夜色而行,
蹣跚地
拖曳謙卑的身影。

# Vagrant

Autumn grasses
spread across his scalp,
his two eyes dry
under withered stalks.
No one can judge
how rich and weighty his soul;
they see only the signs of hunger,
written upon his loose and wrinkled skin
by protruding ribs.

Who is it that failed him?
Or who is it
made him fail himself this way?
Perhaps those of us who should've been charitable,
and refused his existence long ago?
Look at him now, still with a polite air,
take night by the arm and walk
unsteadily
dragging his humble shadow.

## 暑雨

它滿滿地蘊飽了奶汁
像是突然會噴灑出來。

倏然間,天空變成一只大乳房
豐沛的母愛
滋潤了每個嗷嗷待哺的生靈。
那過剩的乳汁
彷彿蛇群一般
竄入這城市的隱形血管,
混雜著原本攝取過多的垃圾食物
直通賁門。

抬頭一看;
天空已是哺育過後的樣子。
藍,乾乾癟癟地貼在上面。

## Summer Rain

It slowly collects milk
until it looks ready to burst.

Suddenly, the sky's become a huge breast,
copious mother love
nourishing every creature crying to be fed.
That rush of milk
like a hoard of snakes
surging into the city's hidden arteries,
mixing with the original mess of junk food,
heading straight for the stomach.

Look up;
the sky's already got that after-a-feeding look.
A shriveled blue pasted overhead.

## 星期五、禮拜二以及星期日

「讓我在妳母性的土地上鑿井。」
這是星期五。一位建築工地詩人說的。
他一天工錢一千六。
走的時候
枕邊躺著3又1/2 天的生命酬庸。

傳教士走了進來,
他的金髮像耶穌一般鬈。
「我以為你們都不會來的⋯⋯」

他說　阿門
以及聖、聖、聖、聖母瑪麗亞。
「禮拜天記得來教堂作禮拜。」
他給了錢。
和憐憫。

星期天。無事可做。
到西區百貨買一支叫「毒藥」的香水。
工地有人喊叫。
一朵烏雲降在前面不遠處,
灑落滂沱紅雨。
啊!是星期五殘留的抽搐
已靜靜躺成最後的十字架。

今天,不是禮拜?的日子?嗎?
忽然想起
該去教堂向傳教士告解。

## Friday, Tuesday, and Sunday

"Let me dig a well in your maternal soil."
It's Friday. A poet at a construction site says so.
He earns fifty bucks a day.
When he leaves
3 and 1/2 days of life's recompense lie beside the pillow.

A missionary walks in,
his blond hair wavy as Jesus'.
"I thought none of you would come......"

He says        Amen
and holy, holy, holy, holy Mother Mary.
"Remember to come to church on the Lord's Day and pray."
He gives money.
And mercy.

Sunday. Nothing to do.
I stop in the Western Department Store and buy a bottle of
    perfume called "Poison."
There are people at the construction site shouting.
A dark cloud sinks down a little ways ahead.
A trickle, a flood of red rain.
Ah! It's Friday's death rattle,
already quietly laid out as the final cross.

Today, isn't a day? of prayer? is it?
It suddenly occurs to me
I should go to church and confess to the missionary.

## 她們被夢著

幾乎是備受呵護的;
即使入夜了,
為了不使她們獲知恐懼的驚悸
只好把她們囚在夢裡。

(居住一層柔軟且瑰麗的國度。)

但她們極端地想冒險,
想一窺其他之外的感情。

紛紛逃離……
枕著她們睡眠的人,
卻開始作噩夢、盜汗
(那人被魘影沉沉地壓榨著,
汗水從他身上支流而去……)

早晨,當她們歷險歸來,
卻看見床上躺著一株乾萎的
玫瑰花。

## They've Been Dreamed

Just about completely pampered;
even though night's fallen,
to keep them from learning to shiver in fear
it's best to imprison them in a dream.

(To dwell in a soft and lovely land.)

But they really want adventure,
want a glimpse of wholly other feelings.

One by one they escape......
and the pillowed sleepers dreaming these women
start to have bad dreams, night sweats
(squeezed by the heavy shadow of nightmares,
sweat streams from their bodies......)

Morning, when the women return from their adventures,
they find on the bed only a desiccated
rose.

# 暗夜

那一夜,月色何其敗壞。
流言從第一街,
快速衝到巷尾
並且追上逃亡的他

他還想辯駁,
天上一些星光
紛紛洩成地面的銀灰慘澹
閃爍在他的眼裡。
他的眼銀灰慘澹,
而且有些顏色
被其他人
憤怒的目光剝落,
形成一種欺騙似的空蕩。

第二天,報紙上說
昨晚月黑風高,一個青年
消失在一灘血池裡……
整條街都被
開了一刀。
路燈死魚般的面孔
默默地喊了一夜的
痛苦呻吟,
直到流言褪盡,
晨光拭淨暗夜的驚悸後
才停。

# Dark Night

That one night, moonlight so corrupt.
Rumors from the first street
surged down the alley
and caught up with him as he fled

He was still thinking of denying it.
Some starlight from above
leaking into the silver gloom on the ground
flickered in his eyes.
The silver gloom of his eyes,
after other's angry looks
had peeled away
some of the color,
now a deceptive emptiness.

The next day, the newspaper says
last night when the moon was dark and the wind was high, a
    young man
disappeared in a pool of blood……
The whole road
opened with a knife.
The streetlights' dead-fish faces
silently screaming and moaning
in agony all night.
Only when the rumors have faded,
and dawn wipes away the beating of night's terrors,
do they finally stop.

## 黑牡丹
──寫給在黑夜中販售青春與美麗的女子們

黑夜的香氣在瀰漫了。
彼時,
用心情深呼吸的人
都聞得到:
悲哀的味道　綠色盒裝的薄荷香菸
疲倦的味道　暈開且失神的眼線
痛苦的味道　剝落不勻的脣色
憂傷的味道　鬈燙而分叉的枯髮
沉淪的味道　桃紅瘦長的指甲
情慾的味道　雜牌香水的放肆
無所謂的味道　洋裝下不著褻衣的胴體

在沉靜的爆烈中,
自巨大的闇幽處,
一朵噬心的黑色牡丹
綻放。

# Black Peony
*—For the women who sell youth and beauty in the dark of night*

The fragrance of night fills the air.
It's then
that those who breathe deeply and with feeling
catch the scent:

of sorrow       a green box of menthol cigarettes
of exhaustion   carelessly drawn eyeliner
of suffering    smeared and peeling lipstick
of grief        the dry, split ends of a perm
of oblivion     long, pink fingernails
of lust         the indolence of cheap perfume
of despondence  a body naked beneath her little dress

In a quiet explosion,
from the depths of a great darkness,
blooms a black peony that will eat
your heart.

## 雛樹

不要用銳利的眼光
剝削我日益薄瘦的自尊。
你們看著
僅僅用黑色的眼球看著
我的身體,
竟變成一種骯髒的黃色　流洩
在昏暗不明的舞臺上。

難道你們沒有發覺;
我的青春在熾熱、封閉的空氣中
大量被蒸發嗎?
是的,
慈悲在這裡是一句三字經,
憐憫和同情
不過是戲謔丟擲的銅板。
當我幾乎完裸地舞動身姿,
如一株冬季裡的灌木時
請不要大聲討論我的胴體
及濃妝之下的年紀。
你們哪裡知道,
用淚水灌溉成長的幼齒,
不曾綻放年輕的花蕊、
而容顏早已木化;
我鬆垮的軀幹裡
只有少少的
十七圈年輪……

# Sapling

Don't exploit my increasingly flimsy self-esteem
with a piercing look.
When you're all watching,
even barely looking at my body
with your black eyes,
it suddenly becomes a filthy yellow     leaking
all over the dimly lit stage.

You haven't noticed?
My youth, in this stifling hot atmosphere, has mostly evaporated.
Indeed,
mercy is a four-letter word here,
mercy and compassion
just copper coins tossed as a joke.
When I dance my near-naked trunk
like a tree in winter
please don't loudly discuss my body
and the years beneath thick make-up.
What do you know
about innocent youth watered with tears,
a young pistil never bloomed,
and a face long ago gone wooden.
Inside my untamed trunk
there's no more than
seventeen growth rings….

## 迷路的基因

智弱的母親,閉著眼
懷起她的第一胎;
一個謎題。

胎兒在羊水內泅游,
不安地吸食
母親憂傷的血水。

母親在黑暗的巷弄
追蹤著那夜的真相。
而「真實」,
在鄰人的牙齒中咀嚼,
成為午後談話的

一口　　痰。

# Gene for Getting Lost

A naïve mother, with eyes shut tight
conceives her first child,
a riddle.

The embryo swims in amniotic fluid,
restlessly suckling
mother's thin, grief laden blood.

In a dark alley, the mother
pursues the truth of that night.
But "truth,"
chewed between a neighbor's teeth,
becomes a gossip's

mouthful of		spit.

## 慾望在夜的暗潮，上岸

在這遊戲裡，
當你未感到無聊之前，
讓我的潮水
在你的岸上
漲
滿

一次。

## Desire, in the Undercurrent of Night, Washes Ashore

In this game,
before you get bored,
let my tide
swell
full
against your banks

just once.

# VI
# 寄給憂鬱的一封信
## A Letter to Melancholy

## 後來,以後

後來,我坐在這裡
寫了一首極端暗喻的詩
給你……

我說:
這一生,我等自己快速成熟,
好趕上你憂愁的腳步。
大意如此,啦,
但我的語碼用得太活潑
你可能會不快地閱讀到一半
而放棄誤解我的機會

因為我在字尾上寫著

以後,你若對我的模仿感覺厭煩,
我便開始憂鬱起來
實際上,詩一寫完的那一刻
我已立即教育自己的靈魂
沉重而低迷;
看吧!
都是你害的。討厭。

## After That, After This

After that, I sat down
and wrote an excessively metaphorical poem
for you……

I said:
*All my life, I've waited for my own quick maturation*
*to catch up with your worried footsteps.*
That was, like, the main idea,
but I was maybe having too much fun playing with language.
You'd probably unhappily read about half
and give up. Or misunderstand my attempt.

Because in the afterword I wrote

After this, you'll seem fed up with this version of me,
and I'll start to worry.
For during the time it took to write that poem
I'd already taught my spirit how
to sink into the doldrums;
Look!
This is all your doing. Ugh.

# 蚌

「我獨自懷抱痛楚
日夜琢磨成一顆完美的
；淚球」
一種柏拉圖式的懷孕，
衍生純白無瑕的苦戀。
且到無法隱瞞，
難以吞嚥的哽咽之際，
才緩緩　緩緩
吐出──
無奈的句點。

# Clam

"All alone, I embrace my pain
day and night polishing it into a perfect
; tear"
a kind of platonic pregnancy,
giving rise to a flawlessly pure, unrequited love.
And when I can no longer hide it,
when it's too difficult to swallow down my choking sobs,
gradually     so gradually
I cough up——
an inevitable, round period.

## 寄給憂鬱的一封信

親愛的憂鬱:
我收到你遠方寄來的感應了。
你說:即使在陌生的地平線,
仍找不到一個相契的靈魂。
甚至連自己的影子
也與你越來越生疏了。
而親愛的憂鬱
我懷念你迷人的睡姿,
還有那陰晴不定的體溫。
我竊喜你仍單身度日,
不過為了排遣
你那無趣且脫序的影子,
在這封信裡,
你會掏出一件熟悉的心情
——我的
影子送給　你。

## A Letter to Melancholy

Dear melancholy:
I've received your response sent from afar.
You say: *although I've reached this strange horizon,*
*I still haven't found a kindred spirit.*
*Even my own shadow*
*grows more and more strange.*
Oh, dear melancholy,
I miss the sweet shape of your sleeping body,
the fluctuations of your body heat.
I'm secretly delighted you still pass your days alone.
But in order to rid yourself
of that dull and wayward shadow,
you can draw
from this letter a familiar feeling
——My
shadow, I present     to you.

## 鬧鐘

他們把誓言的期限定在「海枯石爛」那一刻。以為自此便可以沉睡在愛情的夢境。
沒有人干擾,也無人知曉他們的去處。
他們在彼此的語言裡、眼神裡、情緒裡,作清醒而盲目的旅行。
愛,是他們的目標,也是唯一的墳墓……
他們老了,而不覺老。
還在夢的邊緣,用青春的體力掙扎——時間還沒到呢!
他們,卻醒在「海枯石爛」之前。甚至還找了別人的床,繼續睡下去……

# Alarm Clock

They set the expiration date of the oath for *when the seas run dry and the stones go soft.* They think from now on
they'll sleep in love's dreamy scape.
No one disturbs them. No one knows where they are.
Inside each other's language, feelings, meaningful looks, they travel blindly, but knowingly.
Love, that is their purpose, the only acceptable resting place……
They're old but don't feel old.
They still use the power of youth to struggle at the periphery of dreams—don't they know the time still hasn't come!
But they wake before the seas dry and stones soften. And still they search for someone else's bed
to keep sleeping……

## 冷茶心情

大概是深深地憂鬱了。
直到後來，
你皺眉飲下
卻說給我的快樂聽：
「好茶！」

## An Iced Tea Mood

It must be a deep, deep melancholy.
Afterwards,
you drink with a frown
but still say "Good tea!"
to please me.

## 蟹居

到了我這個年齡,
內心的窩穴
正好可以躲藏一個情人了。
他帶著詩集,
和一扇失眠的窗,
住進來,
夜夜偷窺失防的心事、
竊聽囈語洩露太多祕密。

他的身影是那麼柔弱。
蜷著,半個漩渦狀
神經質且不安地睡著。
只要我的心情稍微不穩,
他便驚懼醒來;
敏感的觸角四處探尋,
關於屋租漲跌的蛛絲馬跡。

我猜呀,
他一定惴想;
這柔軟的心房,
哪天會不會殼硬了,
不再適合舒服的殼居?
否則,
這多愁善感的情人
怎麼總愛說:
自己是個寄居的
潮汐生物?

# Crab Shell

At this age,
the cave of my heart
is just the size for hiding a lover.
He brings a book of poems
and a sleepless window.
After moving in,
he peeks at my poorly defended worries every night,
eavesdrops on the flood of secrets mumbled in my sleep.

His figure is so delicate,
curled up, like half a whirlpool
he's nervy and sleeps restlessly.
If my mood is just a little unstable,
he'll jerk away in fright,
carefully feeling all around, searching for
any clues to a fluctuation in his rent.

My guess?
He must be anxious,
wondering when the day will come
that this soft atrium crusts over,
a shell no longer suitable for comfortable living.
Or,
how can such a melancholy lover
gather enough love to say:
I am tidal animal
living far from home?

## 寂寞一種

落葉是寂寞的肉體。
在季節的生息中
逐漸蛻減喧譁的言語
忘卻遇過的人面。

生命曾經來過,
交代一句臨終的偈語;
此時,記憶如透明之水,
感覺它流動的存在,
但怎麼也參不透
「其味如何」?

明知終要安靜地化泥,
獨自,在枝頭巍巍
猶不肯卸掉生的念頭。
眼看著　最新的芽就要抽出
而寂寞仍未凋零……

## One Kind of Loneliness

Falling leaves are the embodiment of loneliness.
Living in the season
I gradually slough off the roar of language
and forget even faces I've encountered.

Life has already passed by.
On the verge of death, let me explain with a verse;
now, memory is like clear water,
I can feel it flowing by,
so why can't I fully grasp
its "flavor"?

To know perfectly well everything quietly turns to mud,
yet there alone, at the towering tip of a branch
still unwilling to let go of the idea of life.
Eyes watching        the newest bud about to sprout
but loneliness still hasn't withered away……

# 梅雨

「我因疲倦而熟悉死亡的感覺
；像一種午后的甜寐。」

當她向我剖析
憂鬱的屬性時,
我不禁懷疑
：如何去透徹死亡與午寐的差距？

梅雨在屋簷,
整日唱著低調的爵士樂

而後,我與她相擁而眠
並交換彼此的夢境,
(我在她的夢裡,
看見我日漸瘦去的生命。)
我輕輕搖她起來
帶著同病相憐的語氣說
：「我開始感覺某種不安了。」

那梅雨終究下到六月底,
都只重覆著日復
　　一日的午寐
還有不安的愛情；
我…………們…………

# Monsoon Season

"Because I'm exhausted, I've become familiar with the feeling of death
; like a kind of sweet siesta."

When she analyzes my
melancholic parts,
I can't help but have doubts
: how to penetrate the distance between death and a nap?

The rain in the eaves,
all day singing a quiet jazz tune

Then, she and I asleep in each other's arms
swapping dreams,
(In her dream,
I see the daily thinning of my life.)
I softly rock her back and forth
and with a misery-loves-company air say
: "I've started to feel a certain unease."

The plum rains will fall until the end of June,
just repeating that day
    -ly afternoon nap
and an uneasy love;
me......us......

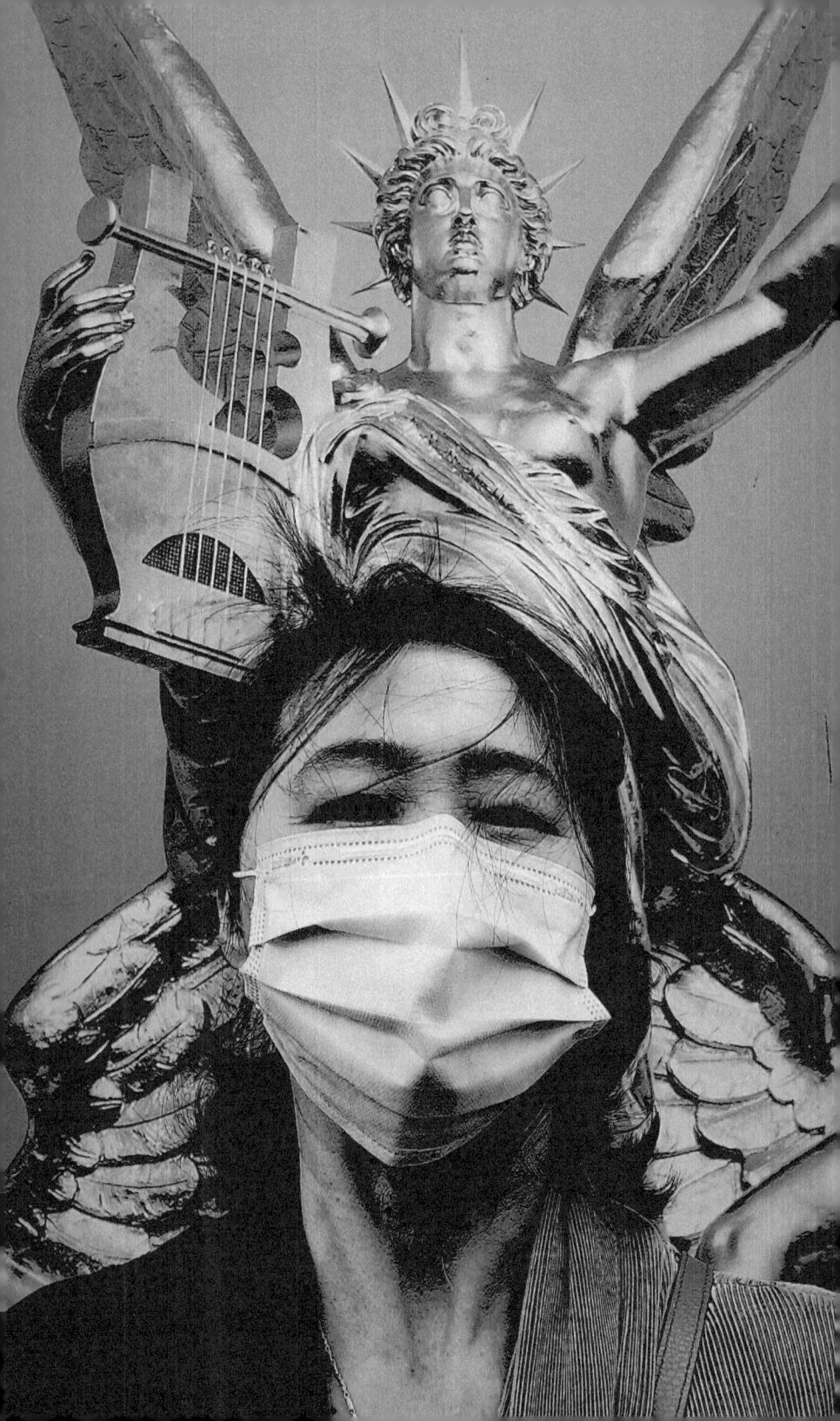

*About the Poet*

**Yen Ai-Lin** is a Taiwanese poet whose work moves between modern poetry, lyrical prose, and cultural criticism. She was the first female poet in Taiwan to publish a sustained series of erotic poems—works that ignited wide discussions on gender and desire. Her writing, shaped by diverse influences, has been honored with the National Outstanding Young Poet Award, the Ministry of Culture's Outstanding Award for New Poem Creation, the Genesis Poetry Magazine 35th Anniversary Poet Award, the inaugural Taipei Literature Award, the Wu Zhuoliu New Poetry Award, and more. Through her words, Yen has left a lasting imprint on readers, on public discourse, and on the study of contemporary literature.

*About the Translator*

**Jenn Marie Nunes** is the author of *And/Or* (2015), winner of the Switchback Books Queer Voices Award, and *Those People*, winner of the 2016 National Poetry Review Press Prize. She holds an MFA from Louisiana State University and a PhD in Chinese literature from The Ohio State University, specializing in modern poetry and film with a minor in Women, Gender, and Sexuality Studies. Her work spans poetry, translation, and scholarship, with a focus on cross-cultural and feminist literary exchange.

www.ingramcontent.com/pod-product-compliance
Lightning Source LLC
Chambersburg PA
CBHW020418080526
44584CB00014B/1385